Working for our Future

Education for All

Judith Anderson with Christian Aid

W

FRANKLIN WATTS
LONDON•SYDNEY

First published in 2007 by
Franklin Watts
338 Euston Road
London NW1 3BH

Franklin Watts Australia
Level 17/207 Kent Street
Sydney NSW 2000
Copyright © Franklin Watts 2007

Editor: Jeremy Smith
Art director: Jonathan Hair
Design: Rita Storey

Produced in association with Christian Aid.

Franklin Watts would like to thank Christian Aid for their help with this title, in particular for allowing permission to use
the information concerning Eduardo and Lalithesh which is © Christian Aid. We would also like to thank the parents of
Gary and Carla for the information and photographs provided.

Picture credits: Adrian Arbib/Christian Aid: 3cb, 10b, 13t, 17, 20b, 21t, 24t, 25r. Alamy: 1, 3, 4, 5 all, 6 top, 7, 8b, 10t,
16t, 22t, 29t. Campaign for Global Education: 16b. Christian Aid/Sian Curry: 25l. Christian Aid/Ramani Leathard: 3br, 9t,
15t, 18t, 19, 24b, 27t. Eduardo Martino: 21b. istockphoto: 6b, 9b, 14, 15b, 26t, 28 all, 29t.
Kim Naylor: Front cover. Ripple Africa: 18b. World Children's Prize for the Rights of the Child: 12.

Dewey Classification 912'.014

ISBN: 978 0 7496 7345 1

Printed in China

Franklin Watts is a division of Hachette Children's Books.

The Millennium Development Goals

In 2000, government leaders agreed on eight goals to help build a better,
fairer world in the 21st century. These goals include getting rid of
extreme poverty, fighting child mortality and disease, promoting
education, gender equality and maternal health and ensuring sustainable
development.

The aim of this series is to look at the problems these goals address,
show how they are being tackled at local level and relate them to the
experiences of children around the world.

Contents

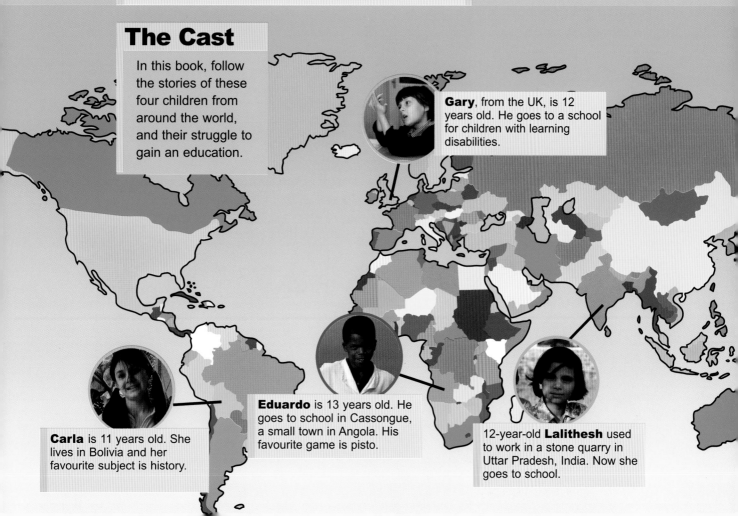

The Cast

In this book, follow the stories of these four children from around the world, and their struggle to gain an education.

Gary, from the UK, is 12 years old. He goes to a school for children with learning disabilities.

Carla is 11 years old. She lives in Bolivia and her favourite subject is history.

Eduardo is 13 years old. He goes to school in Cassongue, a small town in Angola. His favourite game is pisto.

12-year-old **Lalithesh** used to work in a stone quarry in Uttar Pradesh, India. Now she goes to school.

What's school like for you?

Do you go to school? For many children, school is a fact of life. It is hard to imagine what we would do without it. School is where we learn to read and write. It is also a place for playing and making friends. So much happens at school!

Your school

Think about your school for a moment. How do you get there – by bus, or car or on foot? Is it big or small? Is it in a town or a village? What is your classroom like? You probably have books, tables and chairs, pens and pencils. You might also have a computer. Is there a playground outside?

How would you describe your school? Is it a fun place to learn and to mix with your friends?

Pien, aged 10, goes to school in the Netherlands.

❝ I get to school by bus. My favourite subject is geography. Our school has a new gym and I am learning to play basketball. Before we could only do sport when the weather was good. Now it doesn't matter if it's raining! **❞**

School resources

Books, play equipment and computers are called "resources". Sometimes these resources are paid for by the government. Sometimes parents have to buy them. What resources does your school have? Don't forget to include things like musical instruments, sports equipment, kitchens, minibuses and a library.

▲ English primary school children look at books in their school library. These resources are an essential part of the learning process.

◀ Schools in the developed world often have access to the latest aids to help provide a good education. This primary school teacher is using an electronic white board to teach her pupils.

? **Do you think your school has enough resources? Is there anything else you would like for your school?**

Imagine no school!

What would you do if you didn't have to go to school? Watch television? Play football? Stay in bed all day? It might be fun. It might also get a bit boring after a while, especially if your friends still went to school. Can you think of anything you would miss?

" If I couldn't go to school I'd be upset. I'd miss my favourite subjects like art and I'd miss my friends. **"**

Zenab, aged 11

▲ This young girl is working in a textile factory in Hanoi, Vietnam.

Working children

In some parts of the world, children don't go to school at all. Daily life can be very hard for such children. They may work for 12 hours at a time or more in quarries, sweatshops, fields and factories. Sometimes the work they do is very physical, and if they earn any money, it is never very much.

◀ Indian children help an adult transport rubbish.

 These children are ready for their day's work at the silver mines of Potosi, Bolivia.

An impossible dream

Children like the ones shown here are often struggling to survive. They don't have the time, the money or the energy for school. Most of them would love to go to school but they may never be given the opportunity. For them, school seems like an impossible dream.

> " If I couldn't go to school I'd miss our school trip. We've been planning it for ages. We're going to the aquarium! "
>
> **Leo, aged nine**

? How do you think these children feel about not going to school? How are their lives different from yours?

How many children are not at school?

Over 100 million children around the world do not go to school. This is nearly one in five of all children. In some countries, many more children only go to school for a short time. They leave before they have received a basic education.

Per cent
- 30-82
- 83-91
- 92-97
- 98-100
- No data

This map shows the percentage of children in primary education across the world. Many children in the developing world do not get the chance to go to school.

> **❝** The child is entitled to receive education, which shall be free and compulsory, at least in the elementary (primary) stages... on a basis of equal opportunity. **❞**

Principle 7, UN Declaration of the Rights of the Child.

A basic right

Most people, including world leaders, believe that education is a basic human right. A right is something that every person should have in their lives. The right to education is now part of international law. Yet many children in poorer, developing regions are prevented from going to school. In some areas of Africa and south Asia as many as one in two children do not go to school and only half of those who do attend actually complete their education.

This boy is standing in a makeshift classroom in Tibet. He is the only pupil to make it into school that day.

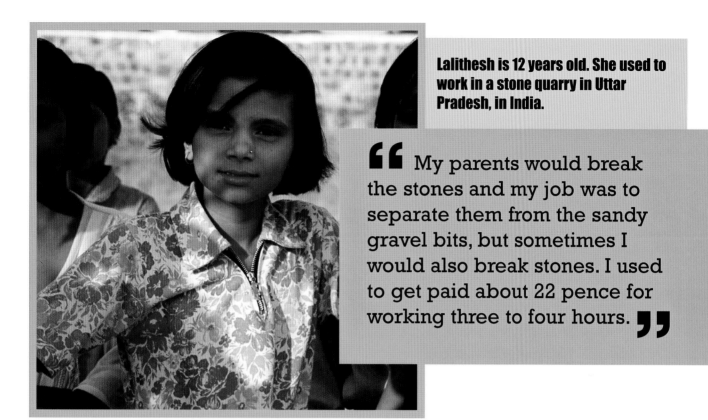

Lalithesh is 12 years old. She used to work in a stone quarry in Uttar Pradesh, in India.

"My parents would break the stones and my job was to separate them from the sandy gravel bits, but sometimes I would also break stones. I used to get paid about 22 pence for working three to four hours."

The problem of poverty

The problem for many children is poverty. Education costs money. Buildings, teachers, books and uniforms must be paid for and in many countries the government does not provide these resources. So some families simply cannot afford to send their children to school. Also, if parents send their child to school then that child will not be collecting firewood, fetching water or earning a wage. Many families depend on their children for these things.

This child in India is picking tea leaves to bring in money for her family. She doesn't have time to go to school most weeks.

? Why do you think Lalithesh had to work in a quarry rather than go to school?

What stops children from going to school?

Poverty is the main reason why many children can't go to school, but it is not the only reason. Perhaps there is no school in the area. Perhaps a child has no parents and must stay at home to look after younger brothers and sisters. Problems such as war or illness can also make it difficult for children to go to school.

▲ These children in Tanzania are not receiving a proper education. They are being taught outside in large numbers.

Eduardo is 13 and lives in Angola. His home town of Cassongue was badly hit by Angola's civil war (1974-2002) and many people ran away to the mountains when the fighting started. Now the war is over. Families are returning and everyone is trying to rebuild their lives.

“ There are 61 students in my class but they don't all come every day. ”

Not enough teachers

At the moment, there is a worldwide shortage of teachers. Classes in some countries have up to 100 children in them. More than 20 million extra teachers are needed if all children are to receive good quality primary education by 2015. For children with special educational needs such as Gary (opposite top), individual attention is needed to help him reach his full potential at school.

Gary lives in the UK. He has Asperger's Syndrome. This means that he thinks in a different way to others. He needed a special kind of teacher to succeed at school.

" Because I can't read as easily as other children, I found schoolwork very difficult. I changed schools several times, but I never got the help I really needed. **"**

Problems for girls

In some countries, girls are often prevented from going to school. This may be because their families expect girls to do the chores like fetching water or tending animals. They may be expected to marry at a young age and have children. Or it may be because parents prefer to send their sons to school. These girls are not being given the same chances as boys.

" I had to work until four or five in the morning. **"**

Carla lives in Bolivia. She was forced to go out to work all day and most of the night by family members when she was seven. Her job selling cigarettes and sweets was difficult and dangerous.

? Why has it been difficult for Eduardo and Carla to go to school? How are their lives different from yours?

Why is school so important?

School is vitally important for all children because it is the best way for them to learn the skills they need to find jobs, stay healthy, stand up for their rights and bring about change in their lives. It gives them the hope of a better future.

Essential skills

Reading and writing are essential skills. Parents need to understand information about keeping their families healthy. Anyone applying for a job needs to be able to fill out an application form and we all need to recognise the word "Danger" when we see it.

Schools also teach us other valuable skills and help us find out about the world around us. A good education teaches us about history, science, art and how to think for ourselves.

Nelson Mandela, the former South African president, receives flowers from Xola Dubula for his outstanding contribution to the "Rights of the Child". He says:

❝ Education is the most powerful weapon you can use to change the world. ❞

Eduardo's favourite subject at school is maths.

It's important to go to school so I can find a job when I'm older.

New opportunities

School means that people can improve their lives. A child from a poor family who has been to school can hope to find a better-paid job or go to college or learn to speak out on behalf of others. Education helps people out of poverty and inequality and sets them on the path to greater freedom and choices in life.

Gary found school difficult, and wasn't learning properly. Then he was given a place at a new school for children with similar problems to his.

Working with my own teacher helped lots. I quickly began to improve at school.

? How can school help improve the lives of children like Eduardo and Gary?

Tackling the problem

In the year 2000, the world's leaders met at the United Nations and agreed a set of eight goals that would help to make the world a better, fairer place in the 21st century. The goals recognise the key role of education in improving the lives of millions of children worldwide.

" Children are going to either get an education and become better people... or sit idle with nothing to do. That's one of the saddest things – to see a little life that in many ways is going to go to waste. **"**

The actress Angelina Jolie speaking on behalf of the Global Campaign for Education

THE EIGHT MILLENNIUM DEVELOPMENT GOALS

1 Get rid of extreme poverty and hunger

2 Primary education for all

3 Promote equal chances for girls and women

4 Reduce child mortality

5 Improve the health of mothers

6 Combat HIV/AIDS, malaria and other diseases

7 Ensure environmental sustainability

8 Address the special needs of developing countries, including debt and fair trade

The goals
Each goal has targets that need to be achieved by the year 2015 and governments have been asked to make policies that will ensure these targets are met.

On target
The second goal is about education. The target is to make sure that by 2015,

children everywhere will be able to complete a full course of primary schooling. Already over 50 million more children are now enrolled in primary school, compared with 10 years ago. However, there are still over 100 million children who are not going to school.

Not just children

The goal of primary education for all includes adults as well as children. Over 800 million adults in the world today have not been taught to read or write. If these people can be given an education even as adults they are more likely to insist that their children receive a proper education, too.

The goal of the UN is to make sure every child in every country gets a start in education by 2015.

" Literacy is the key to unlocking the cage of human misery; the key to developing the potential of every human being; the key to opening up a future of freedom and hope. "

Kofi Annan, former Secretary General of the UN

? Do you think the target for every child to receive primary education can be met by the year 2015?

Bringing about change

Many things need to change if the goal of primary education for every child is to be achieved by 2015. Governments, international organisations, local groups and individuals can all work to bring about such change.

What governments can do

Governments can train more teachers and build more schools. They can also make school free for all children and pay all teachers a proper wage. Developed countries can give developing countries money to help them do this. The benefits are enormous. When the government of Malawi got rid of school fees, one million extra children went to primary school.

▲ In 2005, the president of Mali, Amadou Toumani Touré, signed a pledge drawn up by education groups to "Send my friend to school". The campaign aims to ensure all children get to school by 2015.

These children in Angola are asking their government to do more so that by 2015 every child in the country is taught by a well trained and fairly paid teacher. ▶

Improve chances

Governments can focus their efforts on improving the chances of some of the most disadvantaged children. They can make laws to ensure that girls as well as boys receive a good education and they can stop people from employing children in factories and quarries. They can inform parents about the advantages of sending their children to school. They can also make peace, not war so that children everywhere can go to school in safety.

Children like Eduardo (front of photo) miss school because of the disruption caused by war. Now an international campaign called "Rewrite the Future" has been launched to persuade governments to do more to educate children in war-torn areas of the world.

❝ I saw the soldiers who came here. I knew people were being killed. My family ran away to the mountains. I want to have peace, not war. War is bad. ❞

? Can you think of anything else that governments can do to ensure that all children receive a good quality primary education?

Local solutions

Governments can make new laws and provide money to help more children go to school. But sometimes this isn't enough. Charities and aid organisations are able to get involved at a local level, bringing help and offering support where it is most needed.

A child attends a school set up by the UPGSSS in India (see page 19).

Kinds of help

Some children may have to overcome transport or family difficulties in order to get to school. Others may need shoes, uniform, a hot meal or a place where they can do their homework in peace. A village may have a teacher, but no school. Or it may have a school, but no teacher. Aid organisations work with local people to find the best solutions for the children in their area. In Malawi, a charity called Ripple Africa works with local people to provide an education for children. There are approximately 800 pupils at Mwaya Primary School. They are taught by five Malawian teachers who are paid by the government, together with seven additional Malawian trainee teachers who are paid by the charity.

Children at the Mwaya Primary School receive more attention now that extra teachers are paid for by Ripple Africa.

Better for everyone

Lalithesh used to work in a quarry. Then a local organisation called UPGSSS helped her to go to its school instead. All of the children at her new school used to work in quarries or have parents who work there. UPGSSS campaigns against children working. As well as setting up schools, it also campaigns for higher wages for adults so that they can afford to send their children to school rather than to work.

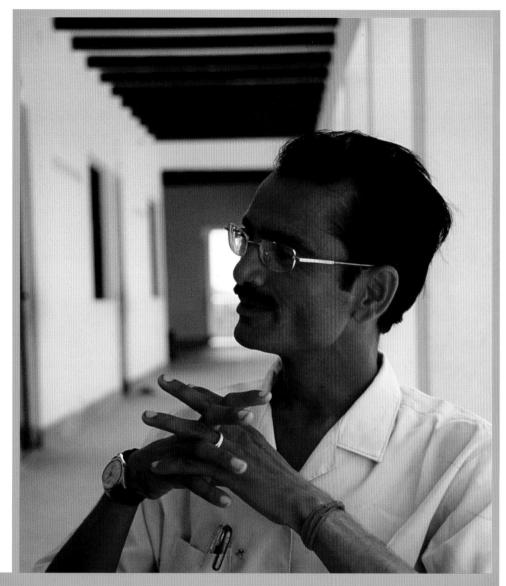

Two years ago I stopped going to the quarry to work because Mr Prem Prakash, our head teacher, said that I should concentrate on my schoolwork.

Lalithesh is glad she doesn't have to work in the quarry any more. She is taught by Mr Prem Prakash (above), who believes it is vital to protect children from such dangerous forms of work.

? **In what ways have UPGSSS and Ripple Africa help improve the lives of children in the local community?**

People who help

All sorts of people are working to achieve the goal of good quality primary education for every child. Teachers are vital. But what about the people who build schools, help with transport or provide school meals? What about the people who campaign for childrens' rights?

" This school is for all children. Their race or their parents' politics doesn't matter. All children have the right to study. Our rebuilding work is helping to bring peace. We are helping people to return home and re-start their lives. "

Julio Luhamo is one of ACM's project workers who helped rebuilt Eduardo's school when it was left without a roof (left).

Rebuilding schools and lives

When war disrupted the lives of Eduardo and his family in the Kwanza Sul region of Angola, a local organisation called Associaçáo Cristáde Mocidade (ACM) helped them. One of the first things they did was rebuild Eduardo's school. His school has even been given a new name – it is called the 4th April School, after the date that peace finally came to the area. Eduardo and his friends are proud of their school now.

These students walk past a tank left abandoned after the war, on their way to school near Eduardo's home in Angola. War was a terrible disruption to the lives of these children.

> **"** Before we had to sit on stones. There's a roof now and we have desks to sit at. **"**

Eduardo is happy to go to school every day.

Making a difference

Charities like Christian Aid support local organisations such as ACM, providing skills, training and money to help them achieve their goals. Between June 2003 and June 2004 this partnership in Angola enabled 540 school-age children to attend lessons. Christian Aid is committed to supporting efforts to protect and promote the rights of children as part of its aim to help the poor. Money from developed countries is channelled through local organisations who can use it to make a real difference.

In El Salvador, Christian Aid's help has enabled children in the poorest areas to go to school, rather than work every day. ▶

? **Why do you think Julio Luhamo wants to help Eduardo and his friends?**

A brighter future

Every child deserves a brighter future. Going to school gives children the tools and skills they need to build a better life for themselves and their families. However, for some children, it does even more than this. It saves their lives.

Child workers prepare for another day's hard labour at the silver mines of Potosi, Bolivia.

Carla's story

Living in a city can be particularly hard for some children. Many of the poorest and most vulnerable end up living on the streets, begging or earning what little money they can. From the age of seven, Carla worked on the streets and in the bars of El Alto in Bolivia, selling sweets and cigarettes. The work was difficult and dangerous, and there was rarely enough food for everyone to eat.

Carla's life was extremely hard and she faced many dangers.

" At night we took a drug called clefa to try to stop feeling so hungry. **"**

A new start

Some teachers from a local organisation found Carla, and asked her to come and live with them in a house for girls who had been working in the streets. Now, instead of working all night long and putting herself at greater and greater risk, she goes to school.

The entrance to Carla's new school in Bolivia.

Things are much better and safer for Carla now she has the chance to go to school.

> I get up at 7 am, go to the courtyard to wash my clothes and then we all make breakfast together. Then I get to go to school! My favourite subject at school is history. I feel very lucky to be able to go to school and when I grow up I think I would like to be a teacher.

? **How might Carla's future have been different if she had not been helped by a local organisation?**

Today at school

What is a typical day at school for you? Lessons, playtime, lunch, games and homework? School children all around the world take part in similar activities, though sometimes they do them in different ways.

Eduardo studies traditional subjects such as English and maths at school. There are no computers so all his work has to be handwritten.

Lessons and homework

In many parts of the world resources are a lot more basic than in developed countries. Lalithesh and Eduardo don't have computers or sports equipment or lots of books. They are taught by a teacher who uses a blackboard and chalk, and do all their work using a pen and paper rather than on screen. Some lessons might be held outside. Some families don't have any electricity in their homes so children must do their homework before the sun sets or in the morning before they go to school.

Lalithesh has a busy day, but still finds time to be with her family and friends.

“ I now come to school at 7.30 in the morning and return home at 12.30. Before lunch I do some homework for about an hour. After lunch, I play with my friends and then come back to help my mother by sweeping the house, washing utensils and looking after my baby brother. **”**

Lunchtime

A free lunch provided by their school makes all the difference for some children. It may be the only nutritious meal they have all day.

> **❝** I get porridge at school. I would be hungry if I didn't have it. **❞**

Talent Nharuye from Zimbabwe doesn't get any breakfast before school, just a cup of tea. Fortunately the free school lunch she receives means she doesn't go hungry in the afternoons.

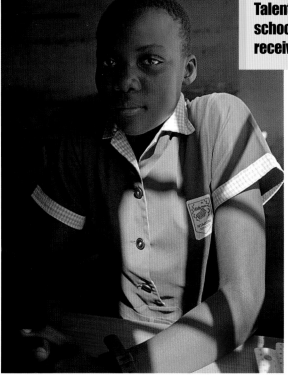

School is great for making friends and learning new games. This is true even if like Eduardo your only toy is an elastic band!

> **❝** Pisto is a game with elastic bands you play with your friend. They flick their band against the wall and to win you have to try to get your band to land touching their band. If you do, you win their band. I've only got one band at the moment. I need to win some games to get a few more. **❞**

? There are many differences between Lalithesh and Eduardo's day and yours. Can you think of anything that is the same?

What a difference!

Now that Eduardo, Carla, Lalithesh and Gary have been given the chance to go to school, their lives have changed for the better in so many ways.

" I like school now! **"**

Since Eduardo's school has been rebuilt, lessons have become more comfortable.

" My new school has completely changed my life. I feel at home and have made lots of friends. I feel much happier about being me now. **"**

Every child counts

Lalithesh, Eduardo, Gary and Carla all feel that they are lucky to be able to go to school. However, they are simply being given the same opportunities that so many of us take for granted. Even though much progress has been made and over 50 million more children are now enrolled in primary school by comparison with 10 years ago, it is not enough. There are still 100 million children who don't go to school. The real difference will come when every single child is "lucky" enough to receive a good education.

For Gary, change came when he found a place at a school that could give him the security and attention he needed.

> **❝** I enjoy being at school because I learn a great deal and have many friends. Also I'm glad I don't have to work in the quarry anymore. My hands used to hurt when I handled the stones. **❞**

Lalithesh is very happy to be at school, along with other children who used to work in the quarry.

> **❝** My dream is to one day go to university and become a teacher. Then I want to come back and help children like me get the proper education they deserve. **❞**

Now that Carla goes to school, she has big plans.

? **Eduardo, Gary, Lalithesh and Carla are all learning new skills because of school. In what other ways is school helping them?**

Action you can take

Do you want to help other children go to school to build a better future for themselves? There are many ways to make a difference, from taking part in global campaigns to raising money and awareness in your local area. Here are some ideas.

Research

Find out more about the Millennium Development Goals by logging on to www.millenniumcampaign.org and clicking on Goal 2 - "Achieve universal primary education". This site has lots of information and links for getting involved in campaigns such as the Global Campaign for Education.

Recycle

Find out about charities that send resources to schools that need them. Some charities specialise in sending second-hand books or basic writing equipment such as pencils and pens. Others recycle old computers, or even send second-hand bikes for use by children who live a long way away from school. Decide what spare resources you have in your school or local community, and start collecting!

▲ Charities such as Books Abroad collect books and other educational materials and send them to help children in the poorest parts of the world.

▲ Visit the UN's Millennium Development Goals page and see what you can do to help.

Raise money

There are thousands of ways to raise money for schools that badly need it. Hold a cake sale. Find some sponsors and get your friends involved in a reading marathon, or a pisto marathon (see page 25)! Build a school out of coins. Put on a play. Then give the ticket money to a charity that is directly involved in helping children go to school.

Write a postcard

Send a postcard with a message to the leader of your country, asking him or her to keep the promises made in the Millennium Development Goals.

▲ **Write to the leader of your country reminding he or she of the promises they have made.**

? How will you help to achieve the goal of a good primary education for every child?

Glossary

Aid money or resources such as food, clothing and books donated to those in need

Asperger's Syndrome a condition affecting a person's social and communication skills

Charity an organisation that uses money and resources donated by members of the public to help others

Civil War war between different groups living in the same country

Clefa a dangerous drug similar in its effects to sniffing glue

Compulsory education where school attendance is required by law

Fees money paid by the families of schoolchildren to cover the cost of teachers and other resources such as classrooms and books

Literacy reading and writing skills

Millennium Development Goals (MDGs) Eight goals agreed by world leaders in the year 2000 with the aim of eradicating poverty, illiteracy and disease and promoting the rights of disadvantaged people

Policy a government plan of action

Primary education a basic level of education, usually for children between the ages of 5 and 11

Resources things that assist development and learning such as books, equipment, food or building materials

Right something which everyone should have

Sweatshop small factory employing workers, often children, for very low wages

United Nations (UN) an organisation of countries from all around the world with the aim of promoting peace, development and human rights

UN Declaration of the Rights of the Child A set of ten rights every child is entitled to according to the United Nations. The website is listed opposite

Find out more

Useful Websites

www.un.org/cyberschoolbus
Go to the Millennium Development Goals for accessible and child-friendly facts about the MDGs. Also useful for information about the work of the United Nations.

www.millenniumcampaign.org/ goals_education
The latest news, pictures, facts and statistics as well as information about what you can do to help more children go to school.

www.campaignforeducation.org
Go online to add your name to the millions of people who support the Global Campaign for Education.

www.sendmyfriend.org
Find out more about the 'Send my friend to school' and 'My friend needs a teacher' campaigns and meet some of the children and teachers from around the world who need your help.

www.savethechildren.net/alliance/ rewritethefuture
This site has information on a Save the Children campaign to give education and hope to millions of children affected by war.

www.netaid.org/world_schoolhouse
Information about real projects that are changing lives in developing countries, helping communities lift themselves out of poverty through education.

www.unhchr.ch/html/menu3/b/25.htm
Official UN site detailing the "Declaration of the Rights of the Child".

Christian Aid websites

Christian Aid contributed two of the real-life stories in this book (the accounts of Eduardo and Lalithesh). You can find out more about this organisation by following the links below:

www.christian-aid.org.uk
The main site for the charity Christian Aid, who help out disadvantaged children and adults all over the world, regardless of their religion.

www.globalgang.org.uk
Christian Aid's website for kids with games, news and stories from around the world.

Index